Driving Home on a Rainy Day

Myrtle Wilgis McDaniel

Driving Home on a Rainy Day

Myrtle Wilgis McDaniel

Pleasant Word
A Division of WINEPRESS PUBLISHING

Pleasant Word (a division of WinePress Publishing, PO Box 428, Enumclaw, WA 98022) functions only as book publisher. As such, the ultimate design, content, editorial accuracy, and views expressed or implied in this work are those of the author.

Unless otherwise noted, all Scriptures are taken from the Holy Bible, New International Version, Copyright © 1973, 1978, 1984 by the International Bible Society. Used by permission of Zondervan Publishing House. The "NIV" and "New International Version" trademarks are registered in the United States Patent and Trademark Office by International Bible Society.

Scripture references marked KJV are taken from the King James Version of the Bible.

Scripture references marked NASB are taken from the New American Standard Bible, © 1960, 1963, 1968, 1971, 1972, 1973, 1975, 1977 by The Lockman Foundation. Used by permission.

ISBN 13: 978-1-4141-0798-1
ISBN 10: 1-4141-0798-6
Library of Congress Catalog Card Number: 2006906277

He made the Earth by his Power;
He founded the World by his Wisdom,
And stretched out the Heavens
By his Understanding.

—Jeremiah 51:15

Driving Home On A Rainy Day

There's something good about
Driving home on a rainy day.
The rush of life slows down a bit
And we look along the way.

The neighborhood slacks its busy pace;
Empty yards, deserted streets,
Families retreated into a sheltered world
Children hurry in from play or race
Barefoot through puddles on the ground.
A dog shivers on a porch
And one with nose outstretched
Inside his box curls round.

Nature silently reduces speed
Except for swollen streams that rush along
Out of their banks,
Through grass and flower and summer weed.
Cattle stand passive, heads held low
Birds disappear, their song now still,
To dry recesses out of the blow
Enduring what they cannot change.

I, too, slow down,
Enjoying the warm, dry car
And the mellow, bluesy feeling of memories
Click, clack of windshield wiper;
A companion sound to swish of tires on wet pavement,
Keeping time with thoughts of home
And books to read and games to play
With time that's heaven sent.

Morning Sky
On A Cloudy Day

A well of deepest blue,
Bottomless!
Encrusted with wisps of purest white
Overlaid by floating pearl gray mist
Darkening to a denser hue.
Light from within
Borders each cloud with molten light.

A fringe of clearest gold,
Brilliant!
Thin shadow clouds go scudding by
To pile in massive bulk
And only golden fingers hold
Apart dark curtains closing fast
To sheath my patch of morning sky

A psalm of purest praise,
Breathless!

Sounds At Two a.m.

Serenade of insect voices
Constant, shrill
Unending litany of tree frogs
Incessant, strident
Deep quiver of mournful owl
Unearthly, weird
Panting dog's breath
Rasping, hurried
Muted rhythm of distant train
Rattles, rumbles
Kaleidoscope of passing cars
Surging, transient
Choir-mastered by local hound
Caterwauling the blues.

Rain Waiting To Happen

Storm clouds build and blacken
Ingesting stray wisps,
Lifting fingers of mist,
Droopy gossamer tendrils
Trail lacy fringe
In a patterned wandering
That neither strays or slackens
But moves across the blue
With unpretentious grace.

Oh, cumulus power!
That takes on the tints and hues
Of gray and gray upon gray.
Defacing backdrop of white purity
That neither overcomes your blackness
Nor nullifies your pregnant hour,
But becomes absorbed;
A part of the whole–united in space,
Deluge waiting for delivery.

Symphony Of The Rain

The rain is like a symphony
Split-splat-plop of coin dots on the sidewalk
Introduce the steady drumbeat of instant downpour.

Urgent tri-cornered bird calls
Clear-fluted-repeated
Mute the timpani of distant freight train's moan.

Water cascading from sky to roof to ground
Harmonizes with the steady hum of the clothes dryer
And swish of rubber tires plowing furrows
Through lakes on black asphalt.

Diminishing in fervor, another note is rendered
The tenor and bass as rain drips
From leaf to leaf to leaf,

Leaving crystal drops that cling
To shaggy cones and needles green
Or ping and pong their way to puddles
To silently ooze into the ground.

The cymbal clang of a neighbor's cook pot
Penetrates the stillness
To sound finale to nature's orchestration.

Aftermath Of Rain

It rained for three days
And most of those nights
On ground dying of thirst
And grass, sere and brown.

But now the sun once more ascends
Through skies of clear molten blue.
The air is close and warm upon my face
Even while the rain is dripping
From the low side of my roof.
And grass, now green and strong
Grows to rapid height
Quite unaware the mowers blade
Will reap its harvest before the night.

Man and animal alike
Wake slowly to resume once more
The pattern of their work and life
Knowing that in another day or two
Their first remark will be,
"Man, do we need rain!"

Journey Through Fog

Fog hangs over the land
A wet gray blanket
Merging with gray concrete road,
Swallowing all but patches of yellow stripes.
It billows and clings,
A thick curtain of murky film
Shrouding my view of front and back,
Generating fear as I creep along.
Danger lurks all around me.
A taillight winks
To tell me others make this journey.
I penetrate the mist to find
That pathless realm hidden from afar
Now stands revealed and all
Surrounding me emerges into view,
As I am given light enough
To travel this small space
Within my fog-bound world.

Thank You, God

Thank you, God, for blue, blue skies
And fluffy white clouds.
Thank you, God, for green, green grass
And tiny yellow flowers.
Thank you, God, for clear, cold water
Reflecting sparkling diamonds
Of golden sunlight over gray, gray rocks.

You gave me a beautiful world to enjoy
Even on days when my soul is darkest gray.
Beauty alone cannot ease the pain
Or dull the hurt
But in looking up and out and around
I am reminded of your love–your care,
Your might power.

Thank you, God, for your creation
Because if you care that much
Your design must include me and
You know where I am and what I need.
I'll wait upon you, my refuge, my help,
My very salvation,
Thank you, God.

There's Something About The Morning

There's something about the morning
When the world is quiet and still,
Just before the sun comes up
The air is crisp and chill.

The grass is fresh and wet with dew,
Tree leaves hang completely still in space,
Squirrels wake to scamper down a limb,
Birds flit from place to place.

Most of the world is still asleep
Wrapped snug in deepest slumber.
My old dog lies stretched in dreams,
Chasing rabbits without number.

Blue jays and mockingbirds appear
To make their morning rounds,
They hop from branch to bush to fence
And even on the ground.

There's something about the morning
Before the sun begins to shine
The time before a sound is heard,
When all the world is mine!

A Touch of Sun

The touch of sun upon my face
Is like the hand of God
Touching my cheek–
Warm, comforting, and gentle
Reminding me of whose I am
Indicative of strength
Beyond my ability to measure
Or comprehend.

Red Buds

The most delightful sight I'll ever see
Is red buds forming on the trees,
Who stand tall and bare in winter gray
Unwavering sentinels along the way.
Now with the fresh warm air of spring
I wait to hear a robin sing,
The red buds wave as I ride by
Like scarlet flags against the sky.
There's joy and gladness each time I see
Red buds forming on the trees.

Gold On Green

There's a bright spot on our lawn today
It's a brilliant, golden yellow
A dandelion is in full bloom
A boisterous, impudent fellow.

Each face has a radiant beauty
It lasts but a short, short while
But the sight in the early springtime
Is a glad delight, and I smile.

What glory after a season of gray
With winter's bare limbs showing
In spite of all that's done to it
It just keeps right on growing.

I love this lowly dandelion
That some folks call a weed,
They hack and grub and cut and pull
Before it goes to seed.

Other flowers will come along
Clothed in reds and yellows
But next year I'll know that spring is here
When I see this impudent fellow!

The Bird

There's a bird that comes a'calling
At the first light of the day,
He thinks it is his duty
To help chase the night away.

He calls in tones so loud and shrill
It penetrates my dreams
And he keeps right on a'calling,
Throwing bird notes in my dreams.

He wakes up all the critters,
All the tree frogs and the dogs,
Every katydid and kitten
As he sits atop a log.

Then when all the world is wide awake
And from my bed I creep
To try to face my busy day
That bird goes back to sleep!

Lush

Lush is the word
For the world this morning.
Gardens half-grown
Fields green
Sectioned by winding
Concrete ribbon road
Bordered on either side
By blue gentians
Beautiful and delicate
Stirring in summer's lazy breeze.

A Summer Morning

I hesitate to start the car
The morning is so still.
The only sounds are mocking birds
And blue jays crying shrill.
A bumblebee is busy
At the flower bed by the wall
Where four o'clocks and marigolds
Respond to morning's call.
The leaves of trees just barely stir,
Dew sparkles on the grass,
The swish of cow's tails, seen not heard,
As through the field they pass.
The cornfield at attention stands
Stalks stretched to greet the sun.
Two rabbits stop to nibble grass
Then to the brook they run.
I hurry onward to my work
The day will not be long,
I'm glad I saw, and glad I heard
God's early morning song.

Dawn Greeters

A single note
Clear, distant, repeated
As if by rote,
First right, then answered
Close at hand,
Another voice in treble time
Alerts the land
From left, then higher still
A jubilant band,
Calliope of bird calls.
Trees stretched
Up and out,
Flowers etched
Against the grass,
Evergreen bush
And tender shrub,
Light breezes push
A zephyr touch,
Late butterfly still
Clothed in majesty,
And me.

Blue Jays And Pine Trees

Blue jays and pine trees seem to go together
Each serving as a foil for the other.
Blue jay seeking shelter
Becomes an adornment
On a swaying branch,
Until,
Tiring of the wind-tossed rhythm
He flies away,
Darting, swerving,
Calling to his mate
To join him across the way
On another pine tree's swaying branch
That offers shelter in return for a song.

On The Beach

Stray white feather
Busy ants-intent-determined
Gentle waves lap and surge against the sand
Ruffling sideways, edging out to sea
Sorting and sifting sand and shell
And sargasso weed,
Debris of wood and weeds
Rock-bound jetties, barnacle-encrusted
Shell-implanted
Silhouette of pine and oak bending
Shaped by wind and spray
Marsh grass on tidal flats
Fish that leap and break the surface
Snatching breakfast bugs
Advancing and retreating waves
Leaving a smoothly-packed strip of
Pure white sand
Framed with an edge of weed and wood
And broken fishing line
Green tangled vines creep down
From shifting dunes
Sand crabs make a hasty exit at my approach
Warm sun seeping into the marrow of my bones
Rocks and sticks protrude
In blackened statement
Sky of palest blue, soft patches of cloud
Pastel hues, subdued
Spears of grass
Reclaiming or else holding
The line against take-over
Of sand.

Scene On A Summer Morning

A cocky mocking bird gives
a saucy discourse
on the joys of morning.

An effusive blue jay
edits the sigh of wind and
chatter of an egotistical squirrel

Father cardinal does a pert promenade
on the feeder roof before
issuing a breakfast, "Come and get it!"

A pregnant spider gorges
on a bottle-green fly
in her corner cupboard web.

And I must leave this sun drenched scene
and give my performance
on a different stage.

Circle Of Summer

Summer is hot and lush,
Days that simmer and sometimes boil
Life seems to stand still
In long, lazy spirals.
The truth is, life is pulsating
Straining every cell,
Pushing, pushing to fruition
Every leaf and pod and blade
No more the fresh baby growth of spring,
Tender and delicate to look and touch.
Summer is mature and full,
Filling every possibility with life
While there is time,
Proving its worth before the season changes
And subtle stirring of autumn air
Signals finalization of those
Promises and dreams of summer.
Before the final day when
Green ebbs to colors wild,
Glorious in beauty unsurpassed.
Even glory has its day
And winter comes
Cold, stark and bare;
A resting time, a finishing up,
Sometimes an end
Before life begins again,
With tiny pulse and stirring of regeneration,
Telling us spring has come

Bursting forth, fresh and new,
Paving the way, rolling out the carpet
For summer
When days are hot and lush
And life is doing its thing.

On A Park Bench

In an hour on a park bench I observed:
A mockingbird dive bombing
Two raven-hued blackbirds
Who completely ignored his attacks
And his cries of alarm.
Another mockingbird sat quietly atop
Green foliage of a drooping bush,
Looking innocent and unconcerned
While tiny cries from a hidden nest
Had her immediate attention.
Mr. and Mrs. Cardinal descended to the grass
From an oak tree overhead.
He fed her seeds from off the ground
And by mutual consent they flew away.
A flashy blue jay came to observe
And soon became absorbed
In mutilating bugs for lunch.
Several starlings swooped and flitted
From ground to tree and stopped to feed
As if too busy to linger.
Pigeons walked along red gabled rooftops
Preening their iridescent plumage
Or strutting side to side on red legs
That danced and kept step with
Their bird chatter.
Students strolled by in summer dress–
Or non-dress according to desire,
Vacation was only days away
The lethargy of school disappeared
In the expectancy of home

And long summer days.
Camera-laden tourists stopped to rest
And catch their second wind
Before proceeding on to look and listen
And store memories to tell the folks
back home.
For one brief span of time
The day stands still
As if to catch its breath
Before taking on the busy activity
Of the next hour.
In that special time of peace
I have time to pray
And realize that I am alive
And life is good.

Summer Storm

A storm is in the making,
The clouds are turning black,
Birds are hovering close to earth,
The leaves are hanging slack.
My old hound dog is on the porch,
All air is close and still,
I faintly hear the lowing
Of the cattle on the hill.

It's as if the earth is waiting
To see what heaven has in store,
The gathering clouds are blacker now
Than they were awhile before.
Suddenly, from out of heaven,
Lightning flashes split the sky,
Followed by crescendos of thunder,
Some way off and some nearby.

Here comes the rain, the first big drops
Plop down, fat and slow.
They soon are falling, thick and fast,
The wind begins to blow.
It's a grand and glorious musical,
With visual effects,
That reminds me in the scheme of things,
I'm just a tiny speck.

In a little while the storm is over,
The lightning disappears,
Bird songs replace the thunder,

From behind the clouds, the sun appears.
As in life, our troubles leave us,
Storms of passion pass away,
When we have peace that comes through Jesus,
We can face another day.

For the God who made the lightning,
And makes the raindrops fall,
Is the God of my salvation,
He hears me when I call,
And if at times I face a storm
When dark clouds try my soul,
He says, "I'm right here with you,
I'm the one who's in control."

Birds In Migration

Brown-feathered emigrants
on annual pilgrimage
Cluster to roost wingtip-to-wingtip
in perfect symmetry
Atop strong wire-like
empty clothespins in a row.
Rapid fanning whir of
winter-driven wings
Burst forth in patterned flight
to once again descend
Filling live oak branches
with hungry guests to dine on
Tender ant vittles interlaced
with minute bugs and insects small.
Then startled flight again prevails
as instinct-driven vagabonds proceed
To some predestined resting place.

Autumn Soliloquy

I love this gentle day,
Skies of palest blue
Fading away into hazy distance.
A merest trail of cloud
Tiptoes over the earth.

Soft, soft breezes brush against my cheek
With spectral touch.
Trees barely move,
So gentle is the wind.

Birds compose soft melodies,
Dulcet lyrics
Blending with the muted rumble
Of my kitten's purr.

I would embrace the day
And hold it close,
A warm bulwark, a reprieve
Against cold winter's
Coming chill.

Bon Clarken

I walked within your forest dim,
A quiet, lovely place,
And gazed in wonder at the trees,
Great giants of strength and grace.
Quiet, undisturbed by traffic's roar
Or humans' busy pace
Each leaf still fresh with morning dew
Lifts up to seek God's face.
The only sound a hymn of praise
From bird's throats opened wide,
A gentle breeze picks up the tune
That bids me come aside.
"Come rest awhile, slow down the pace,
There's a lesson here for you.
Your body's tired, your mind, your voice,
And heart grows weary, too."
I thought about these trees grown strong and tall
Here in this quiet place,
But would they even stand chance,
Out there in life's mad race?
And then I saw some broken limbs,
Whole trees down on the ground,
While here and there a dead one stood,
Though life was all around.
Today there's very little wind
But storms have had their day
And sleet and hail and lightning's flash
Have passed along this way.

"Take a good look here," the tall pines say,
"For far above their scars
New growth, much stronger than the first,
Keeps reaching for the stars."
Even this quiet place has known the strain
Of nature's strongest blast.
And those who bend and ride the gale
Have been the ones to last.
Life will always bring some times of storm.
You can't always stand so tall.
Sometimes you must bend and ride the gale,
Or else you, too, will fall.

Colors

The colors of spring and
The colors of fall
Are vastly different in hue
Each is a herald
Of changes to come
A messenger of seasons soon due.
The misty sweet whisper
Of spring's gentle touch
Clothing garden and bush and tree
Brings to life what seemed dead.
Signs of hope, signals of love,
The promise of things yet to be
Fall's brilliant display
Of scarlet, russet, and gold
Nature dressed in her best
Shouts of harvest
Of garden, forest, and field
Sings of joy, speaks of life
Whispers of winter's coming rest.
Seasons look different
Their task is the same
As I am different from you.
Changing yet for ages the same
The changing of seasons
And the changing of life
Are vastly different in hue.

Lesson In Color

I traveled down a long, long road
On a journey, weighted down by care.
At first the only thing to catch my eye
Was the asphalt, gray and bare.
Then I began to notice patches of gold
Mid cattails, withered and brown,
The goldenrod stood in graceful sprays
Nodding its yellow crown.
Nearer the road where the sun beat down
On grass already sere and dry,
Beds of yellow daisies and mustard wild
Greeted each passerby.
Across the field by a dark green wood
Stood a house, weather-beaten and gray,
The roof sagged down,
The windows were gone,
The porch had rotted away.
But out in the yard, on an old picket fence,
Climbed a rose still trying to bloom.
Its few scattered blossoms blazed red in the sun
A message of beauty in a setting of gloom.
From a spirit that felt down and barren,
A heart that was heavy and sore,
These bright flags of color reached out to me,
I began to look up once more.
The goldenrod blooms by the wayside,
Some folks say it's merely a weed.
And the rose keeps right on blooming
When its surroundings have all gone to seed.
Life isn't over because you are down,

And your dreams lie in dust at your feet.
The colors we fly may catch someone's eye,
Who needs to bring victory from defeat
Learn a lesson from these lovely flowers,
Show your colors, stand up, be a man!
The setting may not be to your liking,
But if you really want to, you can!

Clear and Cold

Clear and cold
Zero degrees
Windchill thirty degrees below,
We gripe and growl and rush
Inside our houses warm
Make sure our plants and
Pets are safe from harm.
We fill our stomachs
Then switch on TV
Would the picture be different
If we were
lonely
hungry
homeless
sick
old
and cold?

Between Twilgiht and Dark

Things begin to look different
When darkness is closing in.
In the gray half light of the evening
Before night really begins.

The woods look dark and foreboding
Each tree standing still as can be
As if concealing a secret
I'm not intended to see.

The meadow fills up with shadows
Looming black, some slanted and long
They'll disappear with the morning
When birds fill the air with their song.
The woods will be cool and inviting
The meadows will look like a park
But things really do look different
In the twilight, just before dark.

LADIES OF THE FOREST

I walked today through a forest glade
Where Jack Frost had nipped the air
I wanted to see how the trees had dressed
For their annual autumn fair.

The maples were the first to catch my eye
In their stunning attire of gold and red
Against a background of deep green pine
One in pure yellow, flung back her head.

Some bore leaves mixed with orange and gold
Others wore green tipped with red.
Which is the prettiest? It's hard to decide
My eyes with such beauty were fed.

I turned my head and there to one side
A ladylike tree caught my eye.
Standing alone, as if shunned by the crowd
She stood, delicate, demure, and shy.

As if in humility, bending aside
Her branches swept low to the ground.
Her more brilliant sisters in varied designs,
She is deep russet, almost a brown.

I looked at the trees in that forest glade
Where Jack Frost her nipped the air
Each dressed in a beauty all her own
For the annual autumn fair.

Weather Report

"Clear and cold," the weatherman said.
I could have told him that before he read:
"Nine degrees above zero,
Windchill, minus thirty degrees."
I pulled on boots that came to my knees,
With a six-foot scarf wound round my head,
It should have been twelve-foot instead.
I ventured out on the ice and snow,
It surely felt like fifty below.
The air I inhaled was so cold it hurt,
And when I exhaled, it hung in a spurt.
My teeth chattered, my chin quivered,
My whole body shook and shivered.
I hurried as fast as my feet would go,
I slipped on the ice and fell in the snow.
My chores completed, I scurried back in,
Thawed out my fingers, rubbed life into my skin.
I picked up my knitting, sank back in my chair,
And that's where I'm staying
Till it's "fair and sunny."

Sunset On A Winter's Eve

All the world is leaden gray
Wrapped in a blanket of death and decay,
Bare arms of trees reaching,
Silent and old.
Pines, silent sentinels,
Unmoving and cold.

As if on command,
The clouds draw apart,
The sun bursts through, a golden ball
Lifting the heart.
Fingers of light reach far and wide,
Pushing the twilight off to one side.

Feathered cloud fronds
In every shade of pink,
Brush round the yellow orb,
To swirl and to link
With shapes like tattered lace
Then drift on with infinite grace.

The light changed around me…
Every shrub,
Every bush and tree
Appeared alive
With promise of what was to be,
Panorama of expectancy.

I looked across and saw you watching, too,
It's fading now– just a little patch of blue.
What a beautiful reprieve
From darkness,
On a winter's eve.

November Days Are Changing Days

November days are changing days
Hints of coming winter encroach
Trying to crowd autumn into the past.
Cold fog permeates and chills
Merging with wisps of stray cloud
Floating by on silent winds
Closing out the sun
Blanketing me in apathy.

Faint whispering breezes send
Messages of coming transition
Frosty harbingers of winter's
Impending hour.
Then before much time has passed
Skies clear to let
Slanting rays of sun approach
Gentle and caressing
To drench me in welcome languor.

November's Sun

November's sun is not like summer's sun
with scorching rays,
burning hot and crisping,
toasting me to golden brown,
stifling my thoughts
until I spend the days
in torpid languor.

November's sun is not like summer's sun
but slanting rays
envelope me to permeate
with gentle caress,
lifting my mind
Until all of me responds
and I am warmed.

My Picture Book

Each time I see the beauty you created
I want to stop and look
I'd like to take a picture
And place it in a book.

There's lofty mountain grandeur
And splendor of the sea
Meadowlands and racing streams
Or perhaps a single tree.

Then I could show my children
And each grandchild so small
The wonders of your creation
From summer right through fall.

Or days when I am lonely
I could take a look
At the beauty all around me
Within my picture book.

Christmas After The Children Are Grown

There are no children in this house,
No hushed, expectant voices
And little hands to pat my face
And ask, "Is it time?"
Not even a teenager
Making "accidental" noises
Trying to be nonchalant
But eager to know
What is beneath the pretty paper
And beribboned packages
Beneath the tree.

There are no children in this house.
Today they reside in homes of their own
All grown up now,
With their own little children to wake at dawn
Eyes dancing with excitement
Happy voices echoing through their rooms.

There are no children in this house
But I am not sad
For you are here and
I have time to think about the significance
Of this day
And offer my gifts of praise and adoration
For your gift of love, the Christ Child.
Better understood because of Christmases past

With family I have enjoyed and
The storehouse of memories I own
And anticipation of more to come.

There are no children in this house
But I am not alone!

Christmas

Christmas is one part memory
Of days when we were young
Of cedar trees and candy canes
Wooden toys and Santa Claus
Popcorn strung and paper chains.

Christmas is one part smells
Of candle wax and fresh cut pine
Of cookies and baking delights
Homemade bread and cinnamon
Lingering far into the night.

Christmas is one part family
Of loved ones coming soon
Of fathers and sons, old and young
Mothers, daughters, and friends
Tales handed down and new ones begun.

Christmas is one part sharing
Of food and clothing and shelter
Of time, money, things we hold dear
With the jobless, the aged, the hopeless
To be given throughout the year.

Christmas is totally God
Of love and mercy and grace
Of sacrifice, our Father's love
Coming to us, given to us,
Immanuel, God from above.

The Heavens declare the glory of God;
The skies proclaim the work of his hands,
Day after day they pour forth speech;
Night after night they display knowledge.
There is no speech or language
Where their voice is not heard.
Their voice goes out into all the Earth,
Their words to the end of the World.

—Psalm 19:1-4a

Words

Hello, I just called to say, "Hi…"
Ladies and gentlemen…
My dear friends…
Spoken words are full of power
Eloquent or scarcely heard,
Every nuance and connotation
Adds meaning to the word.

Dear John…
Dear Sir…
To Whom It May Concern…
Written words–messages to be deciphered
Scanned or eagerly read
Their meaning must be understood
As if the words were said.

"I am the bread of life,"
"I am the living water,"
"I am the resurrection and the life."
The Living Word–God's only Son,
Partaker of both joys and sorrows,
He must be experienced, received, digested
He holds all of our tomorrows,
The "I AM."

Inspiration

There's a poem I need to get on paper
Before it goes out of my head.
Why is it that the words come to me
When I am snug in bed?
If I wait until tomorrow
When I go to write it down,
I discover to my sorrow
All I can do is frown.

No matter how I wrack my brain
In the bright light of the day
I can't recall a single line
Of those brilliant words to say.
I need a special tape machine
So that at night when I'm inspired,
I can simply press a button
That says, "Record–I've retired!"

It's A Boy!

It's a boy!
An accomplishment equal to
Building Boulder Dam!

Breathless wonder!
Equal to
Climbing Mt. Everest!

Miracle of
Overwhelming joy!
Like resurrection morn!

Surging love
Like drums beating
And flags flying,

Just for me!

Hello Out There

I have a time with greeting cards
That say what I want to express,
The verse is on a "Get Well Quick"
When I want "To Wish You Happiness."
I couldn't say it better
On a card for "Wedded Bliss"
Except I want to tell a friend,
"Happy Birthday, Miss."

The picture is just darling
On the "Happy Anniversary"
But inside the words are printed
"With Deepest Sympathy."

So when I want my deepest thoughts
Said with words sincere and true,
I'll simply take my pen in hand
And write, "Hey, I love you!"

Name Quiz

"You have to learn each other's name,"
my teacher said in class.
"And someday soon we'll have a quiz.
It's one that you should pass."

So on our desks we placed our names
And daily tried to place
Some look or act to help us put
The right name with each face.

I learned your names, both first and last,
Spelled each one to the letter,
But one small thing keeps nagging me,
Do I know you any better?

On Writing A Poem
For Class

Written words that start the same
Are called alliteration;
To get the sense right
Requires
Imagination.
Where to begin?
I'm not turned on,
Assonance escapes me.
The sound of words,
The scheme of rhyme,
Simply debilitates me.
Consonance, variety, and onomatopoeia
Sure sound sophisticated.
When I get finished with this course
I'll be emancipated!

What Can I Say?

They say I am too wordy
A fault I must confess
I must learn to tell you
What I think
Or how I feel
In twenty-five words or less.
So with no more explanation
I'll say I'm feeling fine
And I think you're mighty grand.
My words must be compact
Not much between "hello" and "good-bye"
But wait, I find I really must insist
I'll need just one more line.
There'll be no more embellishments
Just state the cold, hard facts.
Therefore, I'll say, "I love you."
That's as plain as plain can be
Before I close I must find out,
Dare I hope that you love me?
No, I must close, they've begun to sigh
And sadly shake their heads.
"Stop! Be brief! Rewrite!
Say what you've got to say.
The very best of writers
Take less than half a day!"
So let me seal this with a kiss.
Then I can say,
"I've said!"

A word aptly Spoken
Is like apples of Gold
In settings of Silver

—Proverbs 25:11 (NIV)

Questions About Prayer

Does conversation with you
Necessitate a prescribed form
Different from how I would talk to others?
Out of ten thousand voices
How will you know it is me
Quoting a singsong litany?
I start to say the words
And rote phrases cascade
From my lips and heart
Like bounding brook water
Over moss-covered boulders
Ripples without much force.
Is prayer simply the pattern I've been taught
Confession, pleas, petitions, thanksgiving
With no two words the same?
Do you really want to talk to me
And not just listen?
Then I must be still.
Other thoughts beckon to me
Until a crisis comes
And calls me to my knees.
Then questions disappear
Into the background,
And only your love answers.

Morning Prayer

Dear Lord,
It's very hard for me to concentrate on you.
I am trying to empty my mind of all but you.
No sooner than I begin to think about you
And who you are
And where I am in relationship to you
Then my mind is off on a tangent.

Thoughts of family, of needs, of work
Sneak into the periphery of my brain
And lure my mind
Like the pied pipers they are.

Half-formed sentences,
Oft repeated phrases
What kind of prayer is that
To offer anyone–
Especially you?

Help me to communicate with you today.
As Holy Spirit, will you hedge my mind
And heart for just a moment or two,
That I might surely be in touch?
Else my day flounders
Just like my thoughts.

Thank you for hearing
And understanding.

Make Me A Pray-er

I asked you to make me a pray-er
But what I had in mind
Was a time of quiet meditation
On a plane, high and sublime.

Instead, I came up with problems
Heartaches too heavy to bear
Troubles piled upon troubles
Made me wonder if you really care.

All I can do is call out your name
Sometimes that's all I can say
But your Holy Spirit takes over
And from my struggles he prays.

I'm learning to pray without ceasing
Means keeping my thoughts upon you
Doing more listening than talking
After confession is through.

You've assured me I could come boldly
To the throne of your marvelous grace
Lord, continue to make me a pray-er
On this day, at this hour, in this place.

Teach Me To Pray

I asked that you would make me a pray-er
But I continued on my way
Of talking to you now and then;
Saying grace, tipping my hat,
Talking about prayer to others.
I even confessed my need to pray more
To my weekday Bible class
And closed the session with moving words
Addressed to you.

I meant them all
And asked again, sincerely,
That you make me a person of prayer.
The days went by and I don't know
How I expected you to answer my prayer.
I do know I made no real effort
To pray more on my own.
Oh, I was busy; both mind and body,
Yet you gave me ample time
To begin to grow in prayer
But I was too busy, too active,
Never still long enough.

And now, heartache has come to me.
Oh, now I pray—with groaning
That cannot be uttered. I agonize. I cry.
Now I am learning what it is
To pray with tears

To recognize my dependence upon you
To see a situation where only prayer can help,
Where only your grace and your mercy will do.

But you told me I could come boldly
That you would give grace to help
In time of need.
The need is not my own
But the need of one I love,
And so I ask–I plead–I beg.
Please help and forgive.
Forgive my failure to do my part
In becoming a pray-er.
Thank you for your work in all of this!
Amazing grace!

Abba Father

I want to run and throw
Myself into your arms
As a little child might do.
I need to cry and cry and cry
Until all the crying is through
I need the touch of your
Strong, firm hands,
As you brush back the hair from my face,
And the comforting sound of your gentle voice,
Repeating your love and your grace.
Would you hold me just
For a little while?
Let me stay and rest.
Let me feel your heart beat in my ear
As I lean against your breast.
Then when my soul is quieted down
Will you listen while I tell
All the things I have stored for years?
Will you really listen
While I voice my doubts and fears?
Tell me once again
Of your love for me.
I know you love the whole world.
But for today, for only this hour,
Let me be your little girl.
When all the talking is over
And all is quiet and sweet peace
Let me stay in your presence one more hour
While you speak words
of gentle release.

After your comfort,
Your love and your grace
Have calmed my troubles and strife,
I can be strong and brave once more,
Able to get on with my life.

My Psalm On Reading Exodus

Put words into my mouth and help me
Learn how to tell others
You want to be their God.
Teach me the patience
Even when I do not understand
The ins and outs of all you plan.
I will be your person
If you will be my God.
Stretch forth your mighty arm
To give me strength,
For you are the Lord,
Mighty, Sovereign God,
The I AM.
There is no one like you
LORD!
GOD!
You are in the midst of the earth
You do not deal falsely as men do.
You do exactly as you say,
Show me your power
That your name may be known
Throughout all the earth.
I will sing songs in your honor.
I will sing songs of praise in your name.
I will remember all of your dealings with me.
I will pass this knowledge on to others
So they, too, can know and remember.

But As For Me

I almost let go
Almost fell beyond all hope
From watching others prosper
Seemingly free from all care and pain.

My pain is real
Despair clouds my thinking
My heart is grieved and
My spirit is bitter.
Do you not see
Or hear their scoffing?
It seems you
Reward callous hearts
And conceited minds.
But as for me
I have no one but you, God.
My flesh and my heart may fail
But you are my strength
Even in my struggle,
My failure to understand or
Find answers that
Stay beyond me.
You are my life
My only hope
It is good to be near you.
Psalm 73

True Worship

The pastor stands in full attire
To lead us as we worship.
Who is this God he talks about
By what right demands our service?

He speaks of all God left behind
When to the earth He came;
From manger bed to sinner's cross
Immanuel is His name.

And now He leaves to us a task
To carry forth the news
Of love that sacrifice has bought
He calls us from the pews.

Into our world, right where we are,
Each one must bear a share
Of bringing hope and life brand new
God help us is our prayer.

Sometimes You
Have To Walk

When you travel by car on interstate or boulevard
Your eye catches a glimpse of homes old and new,
Rivers muddied by springtime rains, tree-lined streets
And open fields, barns, and fences, wild flowers
And carefully manicured beds of marigolds and roses red.
But if you want to sit in the shade of a sturdy oak
Or climb over an old fallen log, touch the lacy tendrils
Of a clinging vine, marvel at the pollen-laden legs
Of a bumblebee, breathe the fragrance of a honeysuckle
Flower before you bite off its head and suck the juice,
You have to get out and walk.

When you travel by car, miles of white concrete
And gray macadam stretch before you over rolling plains
And mountains as old as time.
But if you want to kick the dust on a country road,
Lie down amid the goldenrod, hunt for a four leaf clover,
Have your picture taken by a "Welcome to West Virginia" sign,
You have to get out and walk.

When you travel by car, you marvel at feats of engineering
That blast through tons of jagged rock,
Cutting roads through mountain passes,
Building bridges to span rivers and lakes and such.
And the thousands of men who made such feats possible.
But if you want to climb to the top of a hill,
Listen to the ripple of water flowing over and around
River-polished stones, glimpse the flicker of a mountain trout
Hiding under a grass-hung bank,
Stretch out on a wind-smoothed boulder and

Feel the heat from the sun absorbed by your touch,
You have to get out and walk.

When you travel by car life hurries you along
With a pause now and then,
Just time enough to stretch and sigh and begin again.
But little or no time for minute details or talk
And if you want to look under the top layer,
Feel the ingredients, hear the muted notes,
And consider the reasons and Source of it all,
You have to slow down and walk.

WE MISS YOU

Each Sunday as I come to church
And wait outside the door,
I greet each one as he arrives
To worship God once more.

Today I watched as each one came
Dressed in Sunday best,
I missed someone who's dear to me,
Who failed to join the rest.

"She's ill," they said. "We thought you knew.
She's in a lot of pain."
Each one expressed care and concern
To see you back again.

I bowed my head to quietly pray
That God would give you rest
And give you grace to bear the load
Relief in your distress.

I miss the sight of your dear face,
Your smile and greeting gay,
Please know we love you very much
And pray for you this day.

Trinity

I thank you, Heavenly Father,
Who created me from nothing,
It is your mighty power
That makes me bow in awe.
You give me reassurance,
Create in me endurance,
Enabling me to live from day to day.

I thank you now, Lord Jesus,
Who loved me without measure,
It is your redeeming work
That sets me free.
You give me life forever,
Promise to leave me never,
I owe you more than I can ever repay.

I thank you, Holy Spirit,
Who lives with me forever.
It is your abiding presence
That gives me hope and joy.
You give me peace in sorrow,
Instill hope for my tomorrows,
Rebuke me when I go astray.

I thank you, Heavenly Father,
Thank you, God the Son.
Thank you, Holy Spirit.
Thank you, Three in One.

Query

What did you have for me to do
When you shaped me out of clay?
To what purpose was I born
On that cold November day?

What special niche in the span of time
Did you intend for me to fill?
Have I even come close to finding the place
In the center of your perfect will?

You knew the times when I would fail
Yet you called me just the same
You made me to share your love
To tell, to go, and introduce others to your name.

I'm willing to follow, but on my terms
You know how weak I am.
Ordinary, self-centered, I have little to give
I'm more like a stubborn sheep, not a gentle lamb.

You promise to supply all I will ever need
And be with me to the end.
So here is my life, I give it to you,
My Savior, Counselor, Friend!

Prenatal

What did you know about me
In those days before I was born
What was my place in your planning?
Where would my life be performed?
When you set me apart as your person
To a work only I can attend,
Did you see all my faults and my failures
And still send me forth to that end?

In your ordination for service
To go and tell of your name,
Did you know all of my lame excuses,
My selfish ambition for fame?
Thank you for your confirmation
Your promise to be there with me,
For touching my mouth and my spirit
And sending me forth for Thee.

Four Ds In Life

DISCOVERY
Here I am
Behind the façade of smiles and poise and confidence
Peeking through the cracks of defensive ploys
Searching, yearning, groping.
DISCIPLINE
The hard kind–self-discipline
Taking care of all the oughts and shoulds
The needs and wants and have-to's
Cleaning up the stack of spread-out mess
To file or store or throw away
Capital punishment for all putting off, piling up, or
Dilly dallying until another day
Even love must be decided, debated, categorized.
DEPENDENCY
Upon one who says, "Come unto me."
Whose strength is greater than my own
Who gives hope higher than my greatest expectation
Who walks beside me and not over me to put me down.
DELIGHT
Resting in love that will not let me go
Who says you have not attained but you can try again
In shared laughter
In being in company with others who struggle, search, and grope
In realizing fulfillment is a momentary thing,
Not a lifestyle.

The Mask

Who is beneath the mask
I show to you?
The polished performer?
Do I even know
The one behind the imagery
Or have I become
The one on stage,
My up-front fantasy?

You introduce me
As one you've known
A long, long time.
You don't know me at all,
For all I've ever shown
Has been a visual front
That shut you out
And left my dreams alone.

I'd like to put aside
This masquerade,
To leave the tangled skein of sham
And make believe.
I'm tired of doing life's charade.
I want to tell you who I am
Without distortion or disguise,
But I'm afraid.

Little Bites

Life does not shatter us
in one great blow;
But nibbles in worrisome
bites
That itch and rankle
and ooze and scab
To break apart again
more foreboding than at first
Left untended, they weep
and bleed
Until fragments supplant
the whole,
And only brittle shards
remain
To show what might
have been
Had the wound been tended
when just a wee, small bite.

The Tangled Skein

My life gets like a tangled skein
Of thread or the wrong side of a
Piece of tapestry,
With very little beauty
And lots of knots and tangles
And loose ends.

Threads of disappointment,
Good intentions never carried out,
Deeds left undone,
Good thoughts never spoken,
Promises never kept,
Good news never shared.

But with God in control
My life falls into a pattern
Each thread in place,
Each adding to and complementing
The other–
The warp and woof of all is prayer.

He Makes No Mistakes

My Father's way may twist and turn
My heart may throb and ache
But in my soul I'm glad to know
He makes no mistakes.

My cherished plans may go astray
My dreams may fade away,
But still I'll trust my Lord to lead
For He surely knows the way.

Though night be dark and it may seem
That day will never break
I'll place my faith, my all in Him,
Because He makes no mistakes.

There is so much now I cannot see
My eyesight's far too dim
But come what may, I'll simply trust
And leave it all to Him.

For by and by, the mist will lift
And plain the way He'll make.
Though all the way be dark to me,
My Father makes no mistakes.

Good Intentions

I hope that I will never be
The way some folks appear to me
The smart remark, the unkind stare,
Toss of the head, flip of the hair,
Convey an air of ego tall
Designed to make another small.
As I take stock, this is my plea:
From all of these deliver me.

I hope that I would ever be
The way that God intended me,
Kind and gentle and full of care,
Slow to anger, and quick to share.
A help to folks along my way,
Open to all they have to say.
Easy to say–but hard to be
The way that God intended me.

All For Me

You not only keep my blessings,
You keep me,
Not free from trials and troubles
But you keep me.
There are "no's" that protect me
"Yes's" that guide me
"Wait awhiles" that cause me
To take a second look.

You not only hold my future,
You hold me.
By your great and tender mercy
You hold me.
I have your love to mold me,
Your presence to reassure me,
Your Word is there to teach me
Right from wrong.

I thank you, Abba Father,
For loving me.
I praise you, Holy Father,
For saving me.
I need you there to guide me,
To ever walk beside me,
Thank you for dying for me,
You have set me free.

I Must Speak, I Must Sing

There are statements that need to be spoken.
There are words that need to be said.
There are songs for the hearts that are broken,
The giving of God's daily bread.

There are burdens ready for sharing.
There is brokenness, envy, and strife.
Waiting for those who are caring
To give a new concept to life.

God has given me love for the asking.
He's forgiven me thousands of times.
In His grace and His mercy I'm basking.
My heart rests in peace so sublime

I cannot just take and keep taking
And hold all these blessings for me.
I must do the speaking and singing
To tell of His goodness to me.

Therefore in His name I am praying
So listen with all of your might.
I want you to hear what I'm saying.
You, too, can have songs in the night.

God wants to be your good shepherd.
He is willing your burden to bear.
He is more than able to help you.
He expects me this good news to share.

I must tell all of those who will listen.
I must tell everyone who has need.
I must sing to those who are hurting,
God is for us! That is good news indeed!

To Speak For Thee

If I am to speak for Thee
As opportunity is there for me,
I ask three things of Thee;
Wisdom to speak at the right time,
Understanding to speak in love,
Courage to speak with humility,
If I am to speak for Thee.

The Tragic Flaw

I'm not one to waste my time
I want my life to count
Therefore, I've scheduled all my days
Allotted out amounts
Of time to eat
And time to clean
And time to sew and cook
And in between I worked like mad
My life read like a book.

I scheduled showers and making beds
Laundry and trips to town
From six o'clock to half past ten
My day was written down.
I made sure I put in time with God
To read His Word and pray.
Then I discovered a tragic flaw,
I left no time to play.

The Quality Cleaner

I cleaned up my act
So many times,
Too numerous to mention,
Made promises with hands held high
And resolute intentions.

I changed my ways,
Tried on new roles,
Created new illusions,
But nothing changed,
I just rearranged
My basic mixed confusions.

And then you came.
You cleansed my heart,
Made me a new creation.
You filled my life
With love and hope
When you gave me salvation.

I thank you, Lord,
For cleansing me,
Your love is past my knowing.
Old things are past,
I'm free at last
As in your strength I'm growing.

Not just in words
But service, too,
This news is sought by others;
That you will change
Not rearrange,
And help us live as brothers.

Life Is Like
A Flag That Flies

Life is like a flag that flies.
Some days it snaps and stands out
Straight and beautiful,
Calling to attention those who pass by,
Causing them to stop and salute.
Other days it just hangs there,
Spiritless and dull;
Evoking only a passing glance
Or casual shrug,
Giving and receiving nothing,
Merely watching time's parade.

My Life and the Flag

Some days my spirit cries
And limps along, as if
Marching on blistered feet
With fitful starts and stops,
Saying to passers-by,
"Another day. I'm here but…"

Some days my spirit cries
And hangs wet and plastered, as if
Glued to the mast
Displaying nothing of design or purpose,
Saying to all who notice,
"Today I am hurting, weeping."

Some days my spirit snaps
And stands straight out, as if
At full attention,
Displaying complete color and design,
Saying to the world, "Look at me!
Salute as you go by!"

Thomas And Me

Except I see you in my life
How can I know it's true
What others tell me of your love
Who live and trust in you?

Except I hear you in my heart
It matters not how loud
Another may assert his faith
Alone or in a crowd.

Except I place my hand in yours
In vain I shut the door
Doubts and fears race through my mind
And questions grow the more.

Until in faith I take your word
For things I cannot see
"My Lord and my God," must be my cry,
"Peace," is your response to me.

—John 20:24-28

Coffee Break

I have one quick picture postcard
Space of time
When only God and I are here
And I am one with Him
As in creation
When he looked at the world
And said,
"It is good!"

I Sing The Mighty Power Of God

I sing the mighty power of God
That made the mountains rise
That spread the flowing seas abroad
And built the lofty skies.
I sing the wisdom that ordained
The sun to rule the day.
The moon shines full at His command
And all the stars obey.
I sing the goodness of the Lord
That filled the earth with food.
He formed the creatures with His Word
And then pronounced them good.
Lord, how Thy wonders are displayed
Where'er I turn my eye,
If I survey the ground I tread,
Or gaze upon the sky.
There's not a plant or flow'r below
But makes Thy glories known,
And clouds arise and tempest's blow
By order from Thy throne.
While all that borrows life from Thee
Is ever in Thy care,
And everywhere that man can be,
Thou, God, art present there.

—Issac Watts

My Treasury

I have a house of treasures
That mean a lot to me,
Each piece a glad reminder
Of the way things used to be.

And when Grandma comes to visit,
I see her stop and touch
With gentle hand and happy smile
The things she loved so much.

She can tell the story of each piece
Of glass, or wood, or gold,
From great-grandma's picture on the wall
To a tool chest, scarred and old.

A pair of wooden horses
That rocked each child so small,
A mirror framed with lion heads
On a sideboard in the hall.

There are wedding bowls and a rocking chair
Four generations old,
A shaving mug, old picture books,
Grandpa's watch encased in gold.

When we sit down at the table
We use the same old chairs
That used to grace her kitchen
You should see the look she wears.

Memories that now are hers
She has passed along to me
Of furniture and dishes
That tell our history.

My Kitchen

My kitchen is a wondrous place
Of sink and stove and counter space.
Cabinets lined against the wall
Shelving cans both short and tall.
Spatulas, knives, electric toaster,
Mixer, blender, oven roaster,
Glassware, dishes, nothing old;
Cookware, latest kind that's sold.
Refrigerator shelves full and enticing
Yellow cake with chocolate icing.
Food and drink of every kind
Whatever dish you have in mind.
With all of this at my disposal,
Why do I bring forth this proposal?
Why am I so prone to say,
"Can't we just eat out today?"

Three Meals A Day

If I ever have a servant
Please let it be a cook
Then she can study recipes
While I peruse my book.

Or stay outdoors among the flowers
To work or just to play
If someone else prepared the meals,
I'd gain three hours a day.

Then I could finish what I start
While I am in the mood
And never have to stop midway
To feed my hungry brood.

I'd gladly do the other chores
That make a household run
I'll clean and dust and fold the clothes
And make the vacuum hum.

Meanwhile I guess it's up to me
To prepare and cook the meat
And brace myself for a daily chant,
"Say, Mom. What's there to eat?"

The Grandfather Clock

There's a mouthy old clock
That stands in our hall,
He talks all night
And just has a ball.
He bongs on the hour
And chimes in between,
The noisiest clock
That I've ever seen.

But nights when I am lonely
And need someone there,
I can count on my friend
At the foot of the stair.
He keeps vigil with me
When I can't sleep at all,
That mouthy old clock
That stands in our hall.

Hey, Karen

No longer am I fooled by
Your hard-hearted act.
Last night I saw you
Feed and water the cat
And dog you say you cannot stand,
But when I peeked around the curtain
I saw him come and eat
Out of your hand
And wag his tail in circles of delight.
You thought your deeds
Were hidden by the night,
But I saw you petting them
With tender touch.
The next time you protest
Your great dislike
For cats and dogs and such
I'll laugh at you and to myself
I'll say,
"Not much!"

Dreams

Dreams rise to the surface of my mind,
Unbidden actors playing one-night stands,
Ghosting kaleidoscope of scene on scene,
As stable as a stage of shifting sand.

Are you a fabricated fantasy of what has been
Or prophetic vision of what is yet to be?
Haunting the periphery of my mind—
A costumed reverie.

Fading against the rising curtain of morning light,
Only those few inventions of stark reality remain,
While sneak previews of plots unborn
Float in and out of conscious thought, eluding me.

Dreams, unheralded guest stars of my night,
Are you revealing what my life's about
With run-on lines and misty themes,
Or have I merely eaten too much sauerkraut?

Home For Vacation

The road to home
Stretches endless miles
Beneath my wheels
As I speed forward.
White lines hem in my thoughts
Roadway signs call off how near
And yet how far away you are.
My mind reaches ahead and
Then recoils,
Trying to put together
"Then" as I remember you
And "now" as I will find you
Changed by time and circumstance
And yet still the same,
As I see you
And you see me.
We'll play our games of
"Remember when...?" and
"How is so and so?"
Then we'll settle down and
Be ourselves;
Content to let our feelings show
Until the time comes
When I must leave again
And once more go my way.
Each time
I take more of myself away
Yet leave a residue behind
Just as I carry
Traces of all you mean to me
On my journey
To and from my home.

Place Of Birth

I often visit the birthplace of our country's great men
And review how they lived back then.
I look at their portraits, their hats and their canes
While a docent tells their story again.

Today I visited the place of my birth
In a room filled with cobwebs and dust.
I thought of the two who had given me life
And the way I have lived on the earth.

No historic marker points out the place,
There's nothing of interest to see.
No gowned hostess or plaque tells the tale,
It matters to no one but me.

My heart overflowed, my tears splashed the earth
As I hugged the memories close.
Somehow I gained new courage and strength
As I stood at the place of my birth.

A House On Top Of A Hill

I'd love a house on top of a hill
With the valley spread out below
And a breathtaking view wherever I'd look
In summer's sun or winter's snow.

There might be a farm with horses and cows
Near a house with a wide front lawn,
Or in a pasture that reaches a wood
Where a mother doe stands with her fawn.

Or perhaps a forest with huge green trees
Near fields that are planted with grain,
With contours of gold barley; green wheat and corn
Lifting heads to the sun and the rain.

Over there is a village with houses and stores
And a steeple that points to the sky,
Like a storybook town I've seen in a book
With a river meandering by.

Off in the distance, so far they look blue
Would be mountains ready to climb,
While right at my doorstep, by the fence in the yard
Grow wildflowers in beauty sublime.

From the pale green of springtime to the lush green of summer
Nature will dress the landscape for me,
The red golds of autumn and the gray whites of winter
Keep calling, "Come and see!"

But beauty, like love, was meant to be shared
It can lift the heart with a thrill.
Come, join my dream, and together we'll live
In a house on the top of a hill.

The Call Home

"You had better come,"
the message said,
"Mom's really low today."
Before I could pack
You called again,
"Mom just passed away."

We packed our bags
And sped on our way,
Knowing from other towns
On roads equally long and gray
Others were traveling,
We'd meet at close of day.

Each would bring a memory
Different from the others,
"Remember when…"
"How about that time…"
One way or another
We will be speaking about our mother.

There will be laughter
And yes, we will cry,
No one will love us quite the same
Or lift our hearts and calm our fears
Or be that standby we could count on
That friend of all our years.

We're family–
Closer now, in need of strength
From each other;
Smaller now for one has gone
To be with loved ones gone before
But family, as long as time goes on.

View From An Airplane

Casper ghost clouds trailing wisps of white mist behind
Piled in great heaps like someone gone crazy with Cool Whip
Dirty gray like fine ashes blown across new-fallen snow
Giant scope of snow-like clouds with images of some big-foot
Spirit making dents and furrows
A cloud cove harboring blue mist
Dabs of cotton clouds floating on an air suspension of clear jello
through which mosaics of fields, both green and brown, make
patterns to delight the eye.
Riverbeds ignoring the straight bounds of fields, winding
back and forth in snake-like beauty as if defying man's
neatness and precision.
Running on into barrenness and desert when by surprise
another serpentine flow intersects and waters rush together in
happy reunion.
Lakes of green or blue, like jewels spaced just far enough
apart to draw the eye and break the geometric pattern of
field and road.
Not the cover of cloud or fog but haze of smog and factory
smoke and car exhaust
Not the shine of river or lake but the glitter of sun on
glass and steel.
So many houses in the city–what tears of sorrow, cries of fear, or
shouts of laughter can be heard within your walls?
Water buried deep between steep banks like a ribbon of lace,
unseen unless you are directly overhead where the sun's bright
glint reflects bright and clear, back into the sky
Snow-covered mountains with pine trees showing through like
poppy seeds on white icing

Bare mountain ranges like brown velvet crushed into
valleys and peaks by some giant hand, as one would crumple a
napkinBlack cloud shadows, keeping pace or slightly ahead of
their white fathers,
A dusting of powdered sugar snow over mountains and valleys
making a white lace fringe weaving in and out among deep
gorges and banks of winding streams.
Did some angry god drop his anvil to cleave such gaping holes
or wield his lightning bolts to split the mountains into jagged
monoliths that gape apart for miles on end?
Stone-faced cliffs like toy gravel pits formed by a child
A winding metallic ribbon winks at me from the depths of the
Grand Canyon, signaling its majesty.
A mountain fan-shaped sliding board of wrought brown stone
invites rain to use its face to flow into a riverbed, long dry.
Range of black rock mountains set in a super bowl of white
snow broken by a lone railroad track and toy road like a
pencil mark that disappears in the distance as if the designer
ran out of lead.
A snow-buried town with roadways drifted shut and only dim
outlines to reveal where civilization fights with nature to exist.
Clouds hug the base of a jutting stone mountain soaring high
above its shrouded beginning, looking like snow piled around
a sand castle with here and there a sun-mirrored lake of green
splashing through piles of cotton.
Irregular, jagged, forked, dented, bisected, shrouded, fan-shaped,
every kind of shape
Nothing is the same with God.
Straight lines, square fields, things in a row, even measured
Everything is exact with man.
Impose one on the other
Earth's view is that man has made great strides
Heaven's view–what is man that Thou art mindful of him?

Passage Through A Hospital Corridor

Automatic doors whisper open to let them in,
Eldest son, aged mother, father gray and thin.
Dressed in Sunday best, shoes beaded with rain.
"Step slow. Papa can't move fast."
He holds his leaning side to help subdue the pain.
Speaking softly,
With dignity they walk past,
A fleeting touch to guide
And then she speaks again,
"Step slow. I'm here. Don't be afraid."
Automatic doors whisper open to let them in,
Eldest son, aged mother, father gray and thin.

The Hills Of Home

I stood today on the hills of home
And my heart was quiet and warmed.
I walked the paths where I used to roam
As a child and memories swarmed.

The house still stands where I once lived,
Weathered, deserted, and still.
The road slopes down, weed-choked and steep,
To the stream at the foot of the hill.

A shade tree stands at the old kitchen door,
The latch is broken and gone,
Memories entered the house with me,
The road back to childhood seemed long.

The rooms are empty, the windows are gone
And ghosts walked the roads of my mind
Of family members now grown and gone,
Of pleasures we used to find.

The kitchen porch and Grandma's room,
The front porch latticed and worn,
The wisteria vine and climbing rose
Defy time's inroads with scorn.

The woodshed has crumpled
And lies on the ground, a pile of boards rotting there.
The spring house still stands,
Compact and strong, shelves still intact, but bare.

The weathered shingles of the old gray barn
Lie in a rickety heap,
The pastureland stream meanders along,
Not wide as remembered, or as deep.

I stood today on the hills of home
And my heart was free to roam
As I retraced the footsteps of years gone by
When I returned to my childhood home.

The Viewing

They came to view death
Eyes drawn by some hypnotic force
Fascinated to know
What death had done to you.
What evidence was there to show
How you had looked?
Carefully curious, yet courteous
To give respect to those bereaved,
A quick embrace, remarks inane,
They soon depart, relieved.
Some spoke of death.
"She looks good, so natural,
She seems to be asleep."
What is natural about death?
An emptiness so deep? About absence?
What comfort comes couched in words like these?
What looks good?
The white satin-lined casket
Of dark and polished wood?

I touched death–you never knew.
He imaged your hand in mine
And memory forever holds that feel:
Cold–cold and hard, like polished steel.
Cold enough to burn
Yet, sent my heart racing
Back and forth at such a pace
My breath came raw behind my face.

I saw death clearly and understood at last,
Me–all those who came to view
Your body lying there, an empty shell;
Death rearranges all things new.
No matter how we stand and gaze
We cannot comprehend finality,
Yet I know your immortal spirit is
Melded with mine,
Together, free,
Eternal in eternity.

Vacancy

I looked at a shop today;
Staring blank windows, vacant now
Filmed by passing traffic's dust,
Void and bare–offering nothing.
Vague phantom reminders ghost through the place,
A faint residue of glory awaiting resurrection.
Like a mannequin once dressed in fashion's finery
Strutting its wares in gaudy ostentation;
Now stripped to bare frame and set aside,
So now this square of space
Only suggesting what might have been
And could be once again.

I had to peer past peeling paint, the rusty sign,
Its message long obliterated by sun and rain.
Light penetrating through layers of grime
Reveal accumulated piles of waste
From some forgotten other time.
Walls of faded roses with here and there a tear,
A broken tile, a rusty sink, a worn and easy chair.
I contemplate if I should take a chance
Can this place meet my need? I'll reconsider.

I looked at a man today;
With downcast head he walked the cobbled street
Slouched in Goodwill clothes–dirty and unkempt.
A feeble grin, eyes pleading for hope,
He stumbled, slipped, then stood erect
Striving after dignity long dissipated by shame.
Like my marigold, once burgeoning with golden glory,

Now bowed beneath weight of water-soaked head,
Odorless and brown to the point of revulsion.
So bowed now, this one-time man,
A mere suggestion of what might have been
And could be once again.

I had to peer beneath the cruddy coat, the matted hair,
Empty windows staring in dull apathy–offering nothing.
A fleeting glimpse through mist of morning booze
Revealed accumulated piles of waste
From some forgotten other time.
Shambles of broken resolutions, a shattered life,
Christ died for such as these? Could I meet his need?
Is there time to reconsider?

Putting It Off

How many dreams have gone by the wayside
Cut short by the passing of time?
Procrastination plays a part
As does sickness and the toll of age.
When dreams are young
They seem so attainable
One day soon they will come to pass.
But one day becomes many days
And dreams age
The same as us.

The Drinking Trees

My friends and I know a spot in town
The tourist never sees.
It's not a house of brick or stone,
We call it "The Drinking Trees."

A clump of palms on a grassy knoll
Beside the river's bend,
Where people brown bag their liquid lunch
That makes them less than men.

A sign exclaims in letters tall,
"Lowest Liquor Prices in Town"
But high is the price in human despair
Sprawled there on the ground.

The smell of vomit and unwashed skin
Vie respectively for first place,
While the stench of urine and cheap, sour wine
Are runners up in the "Most Malodorous" race.

Incoherent words and gestures vague
From a brain that's befogged and numb,
Until all of life is reduced to one theme,
"Where's my next drink coming from?"

Who'll bid for this ruined shell of a man,
Empty husk where strength once reigned?
What price do I hear for broken dreams,
Wasted years filled with misery and pain?

If you should be traveling down the road
And this sign you happen to see,
Take a second look and add on the price
Of life under "The Drinking Trees."

What Color Is Love?

What color is love?
Is it gold like the sun
Or is it satisfaction
Of a day's work well done?

What color is love?
Is it blue like the sky
Or is it the laughter
I see in your eyes?

What color is love?
Is it purple or green
Or is it a kind deed
By many unseen?

What color is love?
Is it red like a rose
Or red like the blood
That from Calvary flows

To cover my sin
As black as can be
And make me clean and white
Like my Savior to be?

"Though your sins be as scarlet
They shall be as white as snow;
Though they be red like crimson
They shall be as wool."

—Isaiah 1:18

Be Careful How You Love

Don't love if…
He meets your conditions, because
Your treatment of him
Will be according to your ambitions.
Don't love because…
He is handsome, powerful, or smart.
Competition and comparison
Will eat away at your heart.
Don't love as soon as…
He proves up to full measure,
Meeting your standard
May rob love of its pleasure
Simply love–period!
In spite of…
Anyhow…
For no apparent reason…
Because that's how it is
With God's love
And you.

Deeper Than Words

What does "I love you" mean?
More than the touchy-feely sensations
Although that's a vital part.
More than being held close and
Wanting that to last forever.

Could it be shared laughter over things
Only the two of us understand
And places that belong to us alone
Trusting when circumstances say "don't."
Being silent when you want to talk
Not asking questions
When you desperately need answers
Believing when others doubt.
Accepting differences
Sharing without controlling
Giving of self when the return is uncertain
Sharing innermost thoughts with confidence
Deeper than the words said by so many–
Including the sickness and health
The poverty and wealth
The forsaking of all others–
All of the above
And the realization that each added day
Will bring more understanding
Deeper meaning-but no guarantees.

Love Again

I'm not supposed to feel like this.
Teenage emotions have no place in an old body
A heart that leaps at the mention of your name
That beats like a trip-hammer
At the touch of your hand.

I'm too grown up to be waiting for the phone to ring
And falling apart when it doesn't
To smile at the way you say, "Hello"
To feel the urge to kiss you
When you say my name.

And yet–here I am–in love
Like first love
That breathless, isn't-he-wonderful kind of love
That wants to go for long walks
In the park, on the beach
Or sit and talk or hold hands
Or watch the stars come out.

I'm not supposed to be in love
But I am!

What If?

What if my love is not returned?
What happens then?
Do I cry, scream, plead
Or maybe walk the Appalachian Trail?
An easy task
Compared to the turmoil
I would have to master.
Would God be sufficient?
He promised He would.
Maybe I'll never have to find out.
I need to bury the "what ifs" and
Enjoy the now
Of having my love returned
As long as it lasts.
It could be forever.

Side By Side-yet Apart

I saw our glasses lying side by side
And told the camera of my heart
To capture this picture and
Imprint it in my memory.
More than simply laying aside an obstruction
To being closer to your face,
Your lips–
A picture of growing old together
(because we will grow old
no matter how young our hearts remain)
A still life suggestion of belonging
A rightness of being together
A naturalness
Although casually placed side by side
There seemed a familiarity
As of coming home,
A sense of tranquillity.
But now, we go our separate ways
Looking at our world
No rose-colored glasses these
No mystic images here-
Simply "The better to see you with my child."
I would open my heart for you to see inside,
But I'm afraid-
And I suspect I also speak for you

Decisions, Decisions

When you have to decide if you love me,
Chances are, you don't.
Is love having to consider and deliberate
All the pros and cons,
The ifs, ands, or buts?
The response to such a lot of calculation
May conclude in a chemical equation
But surely not love.

Or is love a happening
An explosion, unplanned, unrehearsed?
An unexplainable flame of desire
That is unabated by time or problems
The need to touch and feel
And answer what's in your eyes
With what's in my heart?

The Telephone Call

I sang as I began my day
Knowing you were going to call me.
And I waited for the phone to ring
Giving fresh meaning to "bated breath."
Lunchtime came and went
And I was glad you waited
Until errands were done and then
There would be plenty of time
And you would say
You thought about me all morning.
I was so sure–
Even took the portable phone to the mailbox
So I could answer on the first ring.
I could have saved myself the trouble
And the feeling I was being foolish.
I reasoned logically with myself,
"He has plans for the evening.
Perhaps he'll call before he leaves the house–
Or after he gets home."
Not really believing that, but wouldn't it be great?
Another day and I hurried through my errands,
Not even wanting to leave the house
For fear I'd miss your call.
A quick look at the answering machine
Yes! It was blinking! You did call!
Only–it was not your voice I heard
I reasoned why the phone remained silent,
"Men don't think like women.
It simply hasn't occurred to him
How much a call would mean to me.

Besides, I'm reading too much
Into this relationship."
And all the while I was willing you to call.
But soon I knew you would not.
A cloud descended on my spirit
But I determined not to cry.
How silly can one be?
Determined or not, tears hovered
Near the surface and then spilled over.
My spirit was crushed.

Then God said,
"Now you know how I feel when you shut me out.
I've waited so many times for you to call to me,
But you pass my love as if it is of no consequence.
You crush my Spirit and don't even know it."
Then my heart was truly broken,
And I know where to give my love;
Where it will be safe and fully returned.
But there's enough left over for you.

If Ever I Walk Away

If ever I walk away
It will not be because I don't love you
Or because I know there is someone else
In your life.
It will be because you shut me out
You keep me on the outside
Wanting so much to be a part of you
To simply know I belong.

So if I ever walk away
It will be because I love you
But I can't go to that desolate place again
Of not counting enough to be included
Or always being in the shadows
Or on the outside looking in.

Reality Check

Reality is hard to face
Cold fact
When "should" battles "want"
And "what if" or "why not"
Fights "no."
And Holy Spirit says,
"Don't you know I live in you?
You can't take me down that road."
Still–it's hard.

Laugh For Joy

Did you ever notice how we laugh
About things and sometimes
Nothing at all?
I think of you and I smile
Simply because you are you
And you make me feel warm and special.
I go to sleep with a smile on my face.
I wake up in the night and it's still there.
I've even been known to laugh out loud
To the amazement and puzzlement of others.
Then I have to make up excuses for
The silly grin I wear.
One should never make excuses for joy!

Printed in the United States
99352LV00006B/1-48/A